Praise for prior parenting and family-formation books by Randall Hicks:

[Starred review] "A brilliantly lean book . . . enthusiastically recommended."
—*Library Journal*

"Educational and empowering. No-nonsense, matter-or-fact advice while using a compassionate approach."
—*Publishers Weekly*

"Showers the anxious parent with information on methods and resources."
—*Booklist*
American Library Association

Featured in the television media:

CBS This Morning, The Today Show, Sally Jessy Raphael,
John & Leeza from Hollywood, Mike and Maty, PBS and
The Home Show

And the print media:

The New York Times, The Los Angeles Times, Chicago Sun-Times,
San Diego Union-Tribune, Orange County Register
and Parents.com

PARENTING

50 One-Minute DOs and DON'Ts
for Moms and Dads

By

Randall Hicks

WORDSLINGER PRESS
San Diego, California

Printed in the United States of America

ISBN: 978-0-9794430-5-3 (trade paperback)
ISBN: 978-0-9794430-6-0 (ebook format)

Wordslinger Press
9921 Carmel Mountain Road, Suite 335, San Diego, CA 92129

PUBLISHER'S NOTE: This publication is designed to provide helpful information in regard to the subject matter covered. It is sold with the understanding that the author and publisher are not engaged in rendering legal or counseling services. Legal and parenting issues discussed herein can be advised about differently, and what is helpful advice for one person may not be helpful for another. If you require legal or family counseling advice, you should seek the services of a licensed professional to serve your personal and unique needs.

Library of Congress Cataloging-in-Publication Data

Names: Hicks, Randall, 1956- author.
Title: Parenting : 50 one-minute dos and don'ts for moms and dads / by Randall Hicks.
Description: San Diego, CA : Wordslinger Press, [2017]
Identifiers: LCCN 2017002270l ISBN 9780979443053 (trade pbk.) l ISBN 0979443059 (trade pbk.)
Subjects: LCSH: Parenting. l Parent and child.
Classification: LCC HQ755.8 .H5193 2017 l DDC 649/.1--dc23
LC record available at https://lccn.loc.gov/2017002270

Introduction

Personally, I hate educational books that are hundreds of pages in length, and by the time I finish, I realize they could have summarized the important parts into just a few pages. Maybe some people think "weight equals wisdom." I don't. I just find the extra 90% of needless fluff to be annoying, and distracts me from the truly important information in the book.

And even worse than that is the result of overly long books. I don't know about you, but many times I start a book, but it is so wordy and cumbersome that I give up before I ever finish, so my time was wasted. Three hundred pages might be great for a novel that you want to slowly savor over your vacation, but a non-fiction book should "deliver the goods" quickly and clearly, and in a way that you can immediately put the information to use.

So I tried to make this book short, insightful and helpful for real day-to-day life. By dividing the book up into fifty DOs and DON'Ts, each with a photo, the 101 pages become fun reading, not with the textbook-feel of some books as if you are studying for a midterm. (At least that's the feeling I get as I read most parenting books.)

As you read these fifty DOs and DON'Ts, there will be some where you will say, "That's great advice, but I already knew that." And also likely, "I did know that, but now that I think about it, I realize I'm not doing it." (If so, I'm proud to be your reminder.) But I can guarantee you that there will be many that you had not thought about, or if you had, that will change your way of thinking. Even one helpful tip—or to look at it in the reverse, one continued mistake in parenting that is not altered—can make a huge difference in your relationship with your child.

But this book isn't just about creating the best possible parent-child relationship. In fact, much of this book is about something else: doing all you can to help your child be happy and confident, and to live with good values, providing the foundation for a fulfilling and successful life as an adult.

For example, one DO gives specifics on how to teach financial responsibility. That's not a subject you'd expect to find in a typical parenting book. You will also read how to get your child to eat green vegetables . . . how to compete in sports in a mentally healthy way . . . how to deal with mean kids and cruel comments . . . and tips on how to make friends.

These are not just issues that impact childhood. They continue into adulthood, affecting personal happiness, self-confidence, personal values, health, relationships, financial security, and the kind of spouse and parent that your child will one day become.

Best wishes and happy reading!

—*Randall Hicks*

Do use "when" not "if."

Ideally, parents are not constantly giving conditions, such as, "If you clean your room, you can play with Hailey." But the reality is that although we try to avoid conditional statements, they are going to occur.

When you do use conditions, always use "when" rather than "if". *If* implies they might obey, or they might not. *When* assumes the child will do as requested. Using "when" shows confidence by you in your child's behavior, and in your authority as a parent, and using "if" does neither.

We are talking about the difference of just one word, but that one word is tremendously important. "*When* you clean your room, you can play with Hailey," sends an entirely different message.

Don't use chores as punishment.

Children will learn to hate work around the house if it's seen as punishment. Yes, the yard may need to be raked, the house vacuumed, or the after-dinner dishes washed, but don't make it punishment. When those activities are chores, fine. But as punishment? No.

A great way to build a good work ethic in a child, and additionally to create a family activity, is to start a family chore day. Maybe once or twice a month you set aside half a day on a Saturday to clean up the yard or the house, or clean out the garage. As the children work side by side with you they see you keep a happy attitude as you work, with a measurable goal to be accomplished, such as a pristine yard when you are done.

And add a reward in the end, like everyone going to a movie together, so the concept of "good work brings rewards" is subconsciously planted. It's a trifecta of good things: You are getting a needed household chore done; you are doing it as a family activity, and you are subtly teaching your kids a valuable lesson. (The best kind of lesson—one that is witnessed in action, not mere words.)

Don't push gender-specific roles on your spouse.

A wife might think discipline is the man's job, while a man may feel discussing emotional issues with a child is a woman's job. Not only are such generalizations wrong simply based upon gender, they can also be counterproductive.

Gender equity not only helps your child within your family, but with life in general. Children will see first-hand that they are not limited to stereotypical roles: that dads can cook and clean and nurture, and that moms can pay the bills, be the primary wage-earner and be great at sports.

Do teach the difference between "need" and "want."

We have become a nation of consumers. We buy and buy and buy. And even worse, many people buy on credit, having to pay the amount owed at some later time. Children, with their lower impulse control, are even worse offenders. So combining the natural inclination of kids, and many adults' poor spending habits, it's a disaster waiting to happen.

Talk to your children about the difference between "need" and "want." Explain how just because we want something does not mean we need to buy it. Often, even waiting a few days after the urge to buy something, a child can see how that momentary urge is gone, or lessened.

Also, rather than replying with "We can't afford it," consider saying "We don't really need it." This is because even if you can afford something doesn't mean you need to buy it. (And let's face it, even we adults need to be reminded of this.)

With older children, start teaching about common sense in using their (or your) money. For example, looking at the cost of something over a one year period is helpful. Let's say your child can't understand why buying the newest model cell phone is a big deal; the cost is only $60 a month. But show them that $60 times twelve months is $720.

For big purchases explain the reality of *disposable income*, which is what you have left to spend after paying for your essentials. Your child might be arguing for a new family car that is "only" $500 a month. He or she thinks you have plenty of money with that big $50,000 annual income. But explain that with taxes, that income becomes $40,000. Pay the mortgage or rent and now it's $20,000 left over. Monthly food brings it down to $13,000. Pay for health care, cars, insurance, debt obligations, et cetera, and maybe you are down to $4,000. This is your disposable income, the amount you can spend. Spend more than that, and you have to go into debt.

So now your child can see that $500-a-month cool new car is actually $6,000 a year, and with the higher insurance for a new car, there is another $3,000. So is it wise to spend $9,000 when your "free" income will be $4,000? So not only is nothing going toward savings—worse, you are going into debt.

Before long, your children will be getting their first credit card, deciding whether to take out student loans for college, and making decisions on major purchases. Helping your kids understand financial responsibility, and how to live relatively debt-free lives, is a tremendous gift to them that will greatly enhance their security and happiness as they grow older.

Don't hide every parental disagreement.

It's often said "don't argue in front of the kids," and that's not a bad rule. However, it would be setting an unmatchable example if a child never sees a single disagreement between parenting figures. A child needs to learn disagreements are a normal part of life, whether it be with a friend or a spouse.

Seeing a disagreement can actually be instructive if the child sees you remain respectful of each other, and witnesses you work through a disagreement and resolve the issue. The message is "Yes, people disagree and don't always get their way, but they can respectfully talk about those issues and try to resolve them."

One thing, however, not to argue about in front of your children is an issue related to child discipline. Those decisions and disagreements should be in private.

Do show love and respect for your spouse.

If you are in a two-parent home, this is one of the most important things you can do to create a happy household. Kids—even in their most self-centered moments—secretly want to see their parents be happy. Nothing will impress a child more about their mom or dad than seeing them love and respect each other.

Remember also that as parents, you are the two key role models in what a marriage should look like, and how spouses treat each other. The "silent lessons" you give in your daily actions will have a much larger impact on your child's life than when sitting down for important lectures.

Do help your child feel good about himself/herself.

Why do we choose certain people as our friends? Why do we want to spend time with some people more than others? Why do some kids like to hang around their parents and some don't? The answer is usually quite simple. *We like to be around people who make us feel good about ourselves.* That is a concept important enough to repeat: We like to be around people who make us feel good about ourselves. This means people we can trust. People who are reliable, honest and kind.

That small piece of wisdom is priceless in making friends—or having a good relationship—with anyone, particularly your own child. Be positive. Be real. Be sincere. Be consistent. Be a good listener. Most importantly, be available.

Don't yell.

Yes, we all lose our temper from time to time and yell, and there may even be rare times where it's needed, but generally it's not the route to take. Have you ever been yelled at by a parent, boss, teacher, friend or whomever? Was your reaction, "Oh, thanks for yelling. Now I *really* want to listen to you." Likely, no. It actually has the opposite effect.

Yelling usually accomplishes nothing but a release of our own anger. So be the calm voice in the storm, and don't add a source of conflict to the behavior that led to your frustration. Adopt the old "count to ten" rule before you react, and give yourself a moment to calm down and think about what you are going to say.

Also, by example you can teach a very valuable lesson in how you react in stressful or challenging situations. A wise old saying is:

> *It's easy to be nice when everything is going your way. But your real character shows when things are at their worst.*

So it is at times like these that a parent must strive to be at their best. If your child learns this lesson as well, it will be a benefit to them their entire life in how they interact with others, particularly during moments of stress.

Do say "thanks" to your children.

Think of all the times parents tell their kids what to do, what they neglected to do, or what they did wrong. It is a wall of negativity and bossiness if you think about it. As parents we often forget to acknowledge what kids do right, except in obvious situations, like a good grade in school, or success at their sport.

But what about everyday life? Give them a compliment for the way they cleaned up their room, got their homework done without you having to tell them, made themselves a meal so you didn't have to, or simply the way they answered the phone or the door.

Also, saying "thanks," to your kids encourages them to copy that behavior, thanking others, not to mention thanking you.

Don't explain.

As parents we want, and need, our children to understand right from wrong, and why certain actions will result in discipline for them. But that doesn't mean that everything needs to be explained. Children can "Yeah but . . ." you forever.

Let's say the discipline method you use is a time out. For it to be effective, it needs to be given *immediately, silently and without doubt.* It is just an automatic result of bad behavior.

Let's say your son has just intentionally thrown a handful of Legos into his sister's face and made her cry. He knows such an action is not appropriate and does not need you to explain it. But he will not go down easily. He's got plenty of ammunition against the unfairness of the time out: "Yeah, but she said I was stupid," or "Yeah, but she threw something at me." The list can (and often will) go on forever if you let it.

Letting a child discuss the "appropriateness" of his or her discipline before it is administered empowers their belief they have the right to question your authority. The appropriate course of action when a child misbehaves is to immediately, and without comment (even from you), start the time out. No discussion by you and no questions/comments from the child. This is hard to do because as parents we *want* to explain. We think our explanation is needed for our child to learn. But the reality is that almost every act you plan to discipline is something the child has already been warned about, or instinctively knows is not appropriate.

However, when the time out is *over*, if he or she *still* wants to discuss it, that's fine, and an explanation can be offered, but only *after* and *only if initiated by the child.* But not surprisingly, when the time out is over, the child's planned arguments no longer seem so important for them to tell you.

Here's a final thought. The term "time out" has been around a long time, and there is nothing wrong with it. But as a child ages, it does smack of something very juvenile. As your child grows you may want to re-label it with a name such as "thinking time" (as in "think about why this is happening"), and rather than have a child sit on the floor as may be the norm when very young, consider altering that as they get older to a chair, but still positioned away from entertainment and distractions.

Do teach how to compete in a healthy way.

Competition in sports offers many great lessons. The joy of winning and the pain of defeat are emotions your children will experience over and over during their lives – in sports, jobs and relationships – so learning to deal with both are critical.

But many parents put too much pressure on their child to win, whether it's a sport, like football, or academic, like the debate team. Not only does this pressure take the fun out of the activity for the child, it is counter-productive to actually winning.

Let's say we have two kids set to run a race. They are told that the winner will be the most popular kid in school forever, and his family will get everything they ever wanted. If they lose, they will be the least popular person in school, and their family will lose everything they own. This is a silly example, but the point is there are big stakes! Big motivation! You've made sure they understand winning is everything . . . so they will *really* want to win, and they will perform at their best! Or so assumes the high-pressure parent.

But wait, that doesn't work. Those two kids set to race are certainly motivated to do their best, but the pressure of such large stakes will almost surely keep them from actually performing their best. Even the best of professional athletes suffer performance anxiety . . . so do we really expect high pressure to work on kids?

If you are a basketball fan, or even if you are not, you likely know who Michael Jordan and LeBron James are. Now they are seen as among the greatest ever in their sport, but in their first few years as professional players, many criticized them for being players with great talent, but who choked at key moments. So do you expect your child to be immune to the very natural pressures felt be even the world's best athletes?

Let's get back to those two kids running their race. Now imagine those kids having only fun motivation, such as the winner gets an ice cream cone, treated by the loser. Now they are motivated in a fun way, and there is no performance anxiety due to high pressure and big stakes. Ice cream is just an example, of course—the point is to make competition fun.

The reality is that no one can control if they win. You can have two great opponents battle, yet only one can win. The losing person may have actually tried harder, yet lost. Both players deserve to feel great about their effort.

The one thing that each competitor *can* control is effort. So the question kids should be taught to ask themselves is, "Did I try my best?" The bottom line is if a child did their best, *and had fun* in the effort, both the parent and child should be proud.

And separate from winning and losing is the importance of good sportsmanship. Often this starts with parents, and how they handle both victory and defeat. Is there goodwilled congratulations to the other team or player for their effort and victory? And if your child is the victor, is that also handled with class? Do you speak highly of the opponent rather than badmouth them? Do you make it clear to your child the importance was in the joy of fair and fun competition, rather than the result?

Show your child these characteristics and they will almost surely copy you and be "a good sport," which is helpful to their success and happiness in life in general, not just sports.

Do choose activities that bond you as a family.

Finding things you enjoy doing together is critical to family bonding. And although watching TV or going to a movie together are fine activities, the problem with them is they are not really interactive.

Strive for activities that will involve conversation and/or interaction. This might be outside activities like hiking or family sports, or inside activities like board games, cooking, a small art project, or creative activities like Legos or K'Nex.

When you think back on some of your most memorable moments with family members, it is likely not a big vacation or huge event. It was more likely little moments, like making homemade cookies with your mom, or playing catch in the backyard with your dad. So fill your life with many such "little" events and activities, most of them costing you nothing and requiring no advance planning. Teach the dog some tricks, decorate cupcakes, shoot hoops, build a birdhouse . . .

Don't buy love.

Buying a gift gives everyone immediate gratification. The child gets a cool gift and is happy, at least for the moment. And you are happy too, not just in seeing the happiness in your child, but likely also (if you are honest with yourself) thrilled with the gratitude that flows back to you. But it's "fast food" gratification.

Gifts are great, but if they are given at the wrong time, or for inappropriate reasons, they are transparent efforts to buy affection. Eventually, both the child, and your spouse, will see it for what it is.

Do give time.

Time is usually our most precious commodity, thus the hardest to give up. The reality is, simply giving a child a present or special treat of some type is much easier than finding free time in a day already filled with a job and household chores, not to mention needing some time for yourself.

But part of parenting is sacrifice. Your child may not give you any credit for it, but you taking part in the thankless tasks that go with parenting (driving your child to his or her various activities, helping with homework, coaching their sports team, attending parent-teacher conferences, sitting at the Girl Scout cookie table in front of the grocery store, or even just giving them your complete and undivided attention while at the dinner table) are the kind of actions that will be recognized and remembered as time goes on.

Don't point out your own attributes.

Every parent has been there—feeling like you are doing too much for others, sometimes particularly for your children, and there is no reciprocity or appreciation coming your way.

This is never more true than when facing the "I am the center of the universe" mentality of most children. It's so easy to want to tell your child the growing list in your head of all that you do for them, usually not thanked or noticed.

But don't fall into that trap. The problem is the "small world" view of a child, and just the way their brains work at younger ages. Kids simply don't have an understanding of the big picture of life, or the world, so naturally put themselves in the center.

There are two specific things you can do to help them see beyond their little world, with them as the sun and everything circling around them. One is to broaden your child's awareness of the world, the unspoken message being that we are each a very small part of something much bigger, in both good and bad ways.

For example, when a news story comes on TV about a catastrophic event like a flood or tornado wiping out entire cities, with families left homeless, invite your child to watch with you (but without turning it into a "how lucky we are by comparison" lecture). And also share joyous and magnificent events with them, such as watching surfers on a monster wave, or watching the sunrise and talk about how it is rising all over the world at different times, waking up billions of people.

A more direct way to create more awareness in a child's home life is to bring up family contributions without referencing them specifically to you. Instead, ask, "What more do you think I should be doing for your mom/dad?" Then, "And how about you? What more could you be doing for your mom/dad to make her/his life easier. S/he works really hard for all of us."

Don't try to be the cool parent.

It's easy to want to get on a child's good side by letting them "get away" with stuff, particularly when you are looking for a way inside your child's barriers. But letting kids slide on rules and responsibilities, or identifying with their point of view even when it's inappropriate, is an easy trap to fall into.

Yes, parents can be friends to their child, but they are parents first. So when the child's behavior is unsafe (wanting to skateboard in the dark), or unkind (telling a "funny" story about a child getting bullied or ridiculed at school), you need to step in and let them know what's right, even if it's not what the child wants to hear. Your child needs your guidance on what is proper behavior and what is not, and in the long term will respect you for trying to teach that. And besides, we all know that nothing is less "cool" than someone trying to be cool, as the above photo proves!

Do be fair and consistent in discipline.

Husbands and wives often have different views on child discipline. And if there are prior marriages and ex-spouses, it gets even more complicated in effective rules for your child. Even for single parents, it can be hard to be consistent, even if it is only you who sets the rules.

Work to develop a fair style of discipline and consistent consequences. Don't treat a specific misbehavior with a laugh one time because you don't want to deal with it, then with harsh discipline another time because there is "time" for discipline, or because you are in a bad mood. And what is considered permissible behavior should be the same for both boys and girls, not a different standard based upon gender.

Don't spank.

Virtually all child-welfare professionals agree that spanking is not appropriate discipline, yet some parents stick to it, often because "it worked on me when I was a kid." The reality is other discipline methods might have worked even better for you, as there is now real doubt if spanking controls behavior at all, and even if it does, is the cost to the parent-child relationship worth it?

Some people argue that the Bible supports spanking, but there is an interesting debate if that is actually true. Spanking supporters cite Old Testament verses like Proverbs 13:24 ("He that spares his rod hates his son: but he that loves him chastens him early."). This is the Bible verse usually cited by those finding support for spanking.

But non-spanking Christians point out that the Old Testament is filled with many stories of violence which are not meant to impart parenting advice. For example, Exodus 21:15 says "If anyone curses his father or mother, he must be put to death." Every child in the world at one point badmouths their parents, yet we clearly don't find biblical support to kill them. Yet many still feel "sparing the rod," is biblical support for spanking.

Non-spanking advocates also point out that the New Testament is "non-spanking." We see that Jesus sought to modify behavior with only kindness and love. He discouraged the Old Testament "eye for an eye" and taught "turn the other cheek." As said in Corinthians 4:21, "What do you prefer? Shall I come to you with a whip, or in love with a gentle spirit?" So the question to be asked is if there is really biblical support for spanking when looking at the Bible as a whole?

Also, laws and perceptions have changed drastically in the last few decades. For example, many people of parenting age can remember that when they were kids, "swats" were freely administered to students by public school officials. Yet nowadays taking a wooden paddle to a child's behind by a teacher in most states would likely not only cost them their job, but perhaps even result in criminal charges.

The anti-spanking sentiment is so strong now that in many states it can be considered unlawful to spank a child, as the line between discipline and abuse can be thin. It is quite humiliating for a good and law-abiding family to get a visit from Children's Protective Services because a teacher or other adult saw evidence of a spanking and called in a report. Simple solution? Don't spank.

Do "edit" your life.

There has likely never been a parent who hasn't said, "There are not enough hours in the day to get everything done." The realities of home responsibilities, family and friends, and likely a job as well, sadly leave little time to really enjoy your daily activities. And this feeling of constantly rushing, and not savoring life, is not only hard on you, but your children as well.

Most adults need to "edit" their lives. Think of it like you are cleaning out an overstuffed drawer, asking "What do I really need?"

One way to do this is to make a harsh analysis of what is truly necessary and important in your life, and what isn't. And since your child's life and schedule is an equal part of your daily "workload," make the same analysis of your child's life. Ask what genuinely brings you joy, and your child joy, and what is an activity one or both of you could do without. The elimination of just one activity can mean hours of "free" time.

If you simply can't throw anything away from your stuffed drawer of a life, another way to get more time and not rush so much is to get up just a half hour earlier. The goal is to have a quiet house while everyone else is still sleeping and there are no distractions, freeing you to get the annoying little jobs out of the way, whether it is paying bills, catching up on emails, or getting a small office or home job completed. Hopefully you can get enough done that it will save you a lot of multi-tasking later and let you focus on, and enjoy, one thing at a time.

Do let your spouse and your child have their own private time.

Shared "family time" is great, but some parents go overboard in feeling everything must be done together. There is nothing wrong with the child wanting—and needing—some private time and activities with just one parent. Special "daddy-daughter days," and "mom-daughter days," and the same with sons, offer special moments for kids.

And it's a perfect opportunity for the other parent to take a day "off," with some well-deserved "me" time.

Do create family activities and traditions.

The more you do as a family, the stronger your family will be. And the more fun you are having together in those activities, the more likely you will all continue doing them, and evolve into new ones as your children grow.

These activities need not necessarily be "big" ones, such as going to an expensive amusement park or weekend getaways. It might simply be Friday night pizza, Sunday morning pancakes at a favorite restaurant, or trips to the park to feed the ducks or do some Frisbee tossing. These "small" activities have the extra benefit of not having any of the pressure and stress that accompanies big events like vacations.

Do imagine the person you admire most is standing next to you when you are at risk of losing your cool.

None of us act perfectly all the time, and there are many times where we've all said something, or acted in a way, which we wish we could take back. This is especially true when the regretted action was directed at our children, or with them watching.

A simple technique to help you be at your best is when high stress moments come to imagine the person you most admire is next to you, watching how you handle the moment. So even though in reality there is no one present but you and your son or daughter, in your mind there is a very important witness to how you choose to handle a difficult moment.

This might be one of your parents or other role model you had growing up. It might even be someone you've never met, perhaps a person famous for their kindness and good character, that you've always tried to emulate.

Do take action with ADD or ADHD.

Attention Deficit Disorder / Hyperactivity is a common problem for about ten percent of children, usually manifesting itself by a child being easily distracted, forgetting assignments, trouble finishing homework or tasks, difficulty understanding directions, and/or isn't able to sit still.

This short segment won't attempt to tackle ADD/ADHD or its diagnosis. But here is one critical thing that is not talked about enough in ADD/ADHD discussions, and that is the loss of self-esteem and self-confidence a child feels when failing or doing poorly in the many aspects of life that ADD or ADHD affects. Experts agree that one of the keys to success in dealing with ADD or ADHD is to find activities or interests that the child truly enjoys. In these activities, many aspects of the ADD/ADHD disappear.

Many of the top entertainers in the music, film and acting communities, for example, have come forward with their battles with ADD/ADHD, and commonly talk about how when they are doing what they love, their passion for that activity seems to counterbalance the lack of focus that is present in other activities.

So to keep your child's self-esteem high when dealing with the challenges of ADD/ADHD, help them find that passion in their lives, where they can more easily match or exceed the skills of others in the field, rather than face continual frustration in struggling in other areas. Give them opportunities to explore many activities: photography, art, musical instruments, sports, carpentry, design, sewing, mechanics . . .

Actually, this same philosophy could benefit all children, particularly those lacking in confidence. Helping them find their passion, and meeting other people with whom to share that interest, can be of great benefit.

Don't be jealous of your spouse.

This may sound ridiculous, but parental jealousy can be a real issue. Children will not always equally display their affection for their parents. Sometimes this is due to the parents themselves, such as if the child sees one parent as more nurturing and meeting their needs. (Oddly, however, sometimes it is the more absent parent who gets the biggest displays of affection, as a child tries to kindle the desired emotion.)

One easy way with young children to balance things out is for the "favorite" parent to let the other parent take over some of the "fun" activities the child looks forward to. When small children demand "I want Mommy/Daddy to do it!" it is also an age-appropriate way to show independence.

But even where each parent is equal in their time and responsibility toward their children, it is common that during certain ages, a child will identify more with the parent of the same gender, while at other times they are drawn more to the parent of the opposite gender.

Regardless of who might be the slightly favored parent at a given time, it is important not to feel jealous of one parent's period of "popularity." Instead, be happy for the great relationship between parent and child. Accept that a child can sometimes identify more with one parent than the other as a healthy occurrence.

What is not healthy, however, is when one parent actively seeks a child's favoritism at the expense of the other parent. This might be giving excessive gifts, neglecting to give discipline for certain behavior as agreed to between the parents, or often saying "Don't tell your mom/dad I'm letting you do this . . ." Even more improper is outright negative comments or mean jokes about the other parent. This is the sign of an unhealthy marriage, and making your child a pawn in the middle.

Do treat sunblock with the same importance as toothpaste.

The importance of brushing our teeth is drilled into our kids from an early age. But by comparison, taking care of our skin by protecting it from the sun is often an afterthought, only mentioned when a full day outside is planned.

Skin cancer and maladies are on the rise with the depletion of our ozone level. Even most parents will admit to themselves they rarely used sunscreen when they were young, and it is only now as they've gotten older that they've realized they need to be cautious with their sun exposure. Don't wait until it's "a problem" before your kids pay attention to taking care of their skin. Be as preventative in skin care as you are with their teeth.

Be aware there are two basic types of sunscreen, those based in *minerals*, and those primarily *chemical*. Google the differences and decide which is best for you. Many health experts recommend mineral sunscreens as they stay on top of the skin and deflect and scatter the sun's rays off the skin, and are normally made up of organic products, rather than chemicals that leach into the skin.

It is understandable that not everyone wants to always put on sunscreen. It can be sticky, some have odors, and the cheap ones can stain clothes. But even just putting it on high sun contact areas like the nose, tops of ears and back of the neck is accomplishing a lot and takes less than a minute. And for girls, often their necks and ears are covered with their hair, so only their nose remains needing sun protection. Also, getting kids in the habit of wearing hats, if they are willing, is helpful, particularly when covering the three key areas: back of neck, ears and face (particularly the nose).

Do find time to focus on your spouse.

It's easy for all parents to get too focused on their children and let their marriage slowly crumble with neglect. There is so much energy going into the needs of the kids there is simply no time or energy left for the spouse.

But just as the relationship with your children would crumble if you neglected them, the same is true of your husband or wife. Also, remember that you are also setting an example for your child that they will carry into their own marriage one day, so openly loving and nurturing your spouse will help both your marriage and your children.

So whether it's an official date night or just taking a walk together after dinner, find some consistent one-on-one time with your spouse. And make sure the "time together" includes a little romance. Little signs of affection at random, perhaps even unexpected, moments, go a long way to keep romance alive: a lingering kiss on the back of your spouse's neck while he or she is cooking, a back rub while reading or watching TV.

And speaking of kissing, when was the last time you had a prolonged passionate kiss (more than five seconds, the kind that would embarrass your kids if they saw it) with your spouse that wasn't during sex? Such kisses are not just for the bedroom.

Do accept your child for who they are.

You as a parent may have genetic gifts or interests that are completely different from your child's. You may like sports, yet your child prefers to read. Or you are an academic but your child has little interest in anything not involving a ball to throw, kick or hit. Maybe you are confident and outgoing and your child is quiet and shy.

Share your interests and maybe your child will embrace them, but if not, accept it in good cheer and sincerely support the unique interests of your child. Let your child overhear you bragging to others about their special skills and accomplishments, whatever they might be.

Do take care of yourself.

The very fact you are reading this book shows you are committed toward your children. That may also mean you are like many parents who spend so much time and energy taking care of their spouse and children that you forget about yourself. Doing this too often, for too long, can actually set a bad example in your family, that mom (or dad) has no life outside the house and work, and it can also lead to some resentment on your part as the years go on.

So remember that it's okay to take an afternoon off now and then to do what gives you peace of mind and pleasure, whether it's just some alone time, or a day out with friends for lunch or some tennis, golf, yoga or whatever. Just as you support your family, they should support you.

DO build a family website or Facebook page.

It's the rare child who does not like being on a computer, regardless of their age. Propose starting a family Facebook page or website to post photos and thoughts to share with friends and relatives. Just type "free websites" in a search engine like Google to find the countless free website options available, or consider a social media like Facebook. Neither option requires much in the way of computer skills, but does allow a lot of creativity on the part of you and your child. Taking pictures, selecting which ones to use and what stories and adventures to share can be fun and a real family-strengthening activity.

Don't get sucked in to arguments between siblings.

It is almost guaranteed that siblings will find something to argue about. Usually this results in the them seeking the support of one or both parents.

Try to avoid feeling you always need to be the problem solver. Instead, avoid taking sides and frame their argument for them as you see it, and give them a framework in which to resolve the issue themselves. "So Jessica, you're mad because Suzie gets in the bathroom first in the morning and you think she takes too long. And Suzie, you are mad because Jessica is banging on the door and bothering you when you feel it's your time in the bathroom. How about you two talk it out and give me a solution during dinner."

Many times there is no significant dispute to resolve, just typical childhood emotions and tension that is natural when sharing space. Also, simply letting the moment of tension pass is often enough to defuse the dispute. With time, and the realization that the parents are not going to "solve" the problem, kids get the idea they are expected to solve their own disputes. The arguments won't completely disappear, but gradually the parents get dragged into fewer of them.

Do teach your child to make friends.

Some kids have the natural gift of making friends, but some don't, and it's painful for both parent and child. There are some specific things you can do to help, however, and the younger your child is when you start, the better.

To learn more than what you see from your own observations, privately talk to your child's teachers who can bluntly tell you what they observe. Oftentimes it's attributed to being "shy," but sometimes there is some behavior by your child that you can counsel him or her about (not sharing, being too physical, saying mean things, declining to join activities).

Most often the problem is a battle with what we generally refer to as shyness. But what is shyness? Usually it is uncertainty or inexperience in how to act with other kids, or some social anxiety. You can help with these things.

It is very beneficial for your child to learn about how to interact with others not only from your words, but by your example. Do you have gatherings (neighbors, relatives, coworkers or friends) at your home, giving your child a chance to observe you being social? And showing that you *want* to be social and you enjoy it? When these get-togethers are at your home they are doubly beneficial as your child is on home turf, so he or she will be more comfortable. So to help your child "learn" to be more social, you might find you need to push yourself as well.

These get-togethers need not be full-out parties, rather simply having friends over to watch a sports event on TV, have a barbeque, or have a glass of wine or soft drink. When their kids come over for these gatherings as well, even better.

If socializing like that is outside your comfort zone, how about letting your child at least observe you in natural friendly interaction, such as chatting with neighbors whenever possible, rather than just encasing yourself in your home. Make your neighbors your friends. Don't be one of those people who drive into their garage and are rarely seen outside their house. Take walks in your neighborhood or putter in your front yard and have an excuse to engage with neighbors. Do you know and interact with at least the neighbor on either side of you, and the houses directly across the street (or apartments across the hallway)?

If not, maybe you can see why your child struggles with easy social interaction.

When you go to the park to supervise your child playing, do you stand off by yourself, or do you start up a conversation with other parents? Not only does your child see you acting in a social manner for them to copy, but it makes it more likely that parent's child and yours will end up interacting more while playing.

Make sure that when other kids come to play at your house that you make them feel welcome, and give your child the skills to make those visits successful. For example, explain how having some games and activities ready is helpful, and the importance of being a good host by letting friends and visitors choose which activities they'd like to do. Some kids feel very awkward initially with new kids over, so start out by adults and kids together playing a game or doing some activity to break the ice.

Signing your child up for a sports team can be a great way to gently force them into interacting with others and bonding as a team. (But make sure you find a level where your child will not feel over-matched.) Joining school clubs and other organizations (Boy Scouts, Girl Scouts, Indian Guides, et cetera) can be very helpful as well.

And make sure you don't set expectations too high. The goal is not to be "popular," but instead to simply have friends to spend time with, both at home and at school. Actually, one really good friend is all anyone needs—and the result of having one friend usually leads to adding more.

Do give easy opportunities to talk.

Some children enjoy an official "family talk time," such as "pass the spoon" where the spoon holder gets to give their thoughts without fear of consequences in a family roundtable.

But other kids may feel it is too forced to share their feelings in such a formal "talk" session, and find it much easier when doing everyday activities (while working together to prepare dinner, setting the table, washing the dishes afterwards, driving to school, et cetera). Mealtimes are also an excellent time to share, so it's a great policy to keep the TV and cell phones off while you eat. Lives can be hectic and busy, but try to select at least one meal a day that is shared as a family and isn't rushed.

Do teach respect.

Parents teach respect by showing respect. Ask yourself, do you treat your spouse, siblings, and your own parents (your child's grandparents) with respect? Or do you argue with them or say bad things about them when they are not present?

And what about respect for your children? Showing respect is a two-way street. For example, do you use sarcasm? The humor of sarcasm is often lost on children. Most sarcasm is actually thinly veiled hostility, and will be interpreted that way by most children. Are you courteous to their friends, or treat them as less important compared to your adult friends?

It is also important for your children to see you being respectful outside your home, particularly with other people with whom there is no personal benefit to being nice, so your kindness and respect is given just because it is the right thing to do.

When you see an older person or a child needing assistance, do you walk or drive by and assume someone else will lend a hand, or do you take a moment to offer your help? This could be something as simple as offering to help a senior citizen lift something heavy into their car in the grocery store parking lot, or holding the door open for someone and give them a friendly "hello."

And what about people in the service industry who are often taken for granted and treated less than politely, such as a food server or a cashier? Do your children see you politely engage with them, exchanging some brief pleasant conversation, or do you just accept their service and walk away without at least a sincere "thank you"?

So to teach your children to show respect to others, treat them and their friends with respect, and allow your children to see you sincerely treat others, even strangers, with kindness and respect.

Do encourage reading.

Reading is one of the most important skills a child, and an adult, can have. You want to nourish reading as a key activity for several reasons. For academic success, good reading skills are essential, and this is true in most jobs as well. Few jobs don't involve reading and writing. (And the more someone reads, the better writer they tend to me.)

But the biggest value of reading isn't related to more success in school and work, rather life in general. A person who always has a book to enjoy is a person who never lacks for something to do. Also, many books have underlying lessons, like overcoming adversity, how to win or lose with grace, dealing with issues like personal problems, from anxiety to obesity to gender issues.

To encourage reading for your child, find books which are in their area of interest. For example, to encourage a child who is only interested in playing sports to read, look at the books by authors like Mike Lupica and John Feinstein, who have novels for grade-school-aged kids to teenagers, and about every sport, from swimming to football. And for older kids, authors like John Green and Jennifer Niven are not only entertaining but insightful on teenage life. Talk to the children's librarian for suggestions, or the staff at a local bookstore. Google searches for categories like: "best grade school fiction" or "best young adult mystery" will give you lots of results. Goodreads.com also has many reader-generated suggestions.

One of the biggest ways to encourage reading is to see *you* reading—not magazines, but actual books—whether fiction or non-fiction, and letting your son or daughter see how you sometimes choose reading over watching TV as your preferred activity.

Do consider attending worship together.

Whether you are Presbyterian, Catholic, Mormon, Jewish, Buddhist, Muslim or ?, worshiping as a family can be beneficial. And if you are a family without a faith, remember that virtually every mainstream religion has the basic tenets of honesty and kindness toward others as principal values, certainly part of something you'd like your child to be exposed to.

It is also a great way for your child to meet other kids and become friends with children whose families have the same values as you. Your day of worship can include small traditions that are fun, such as a big Sunday breakfast at a restaurant, or just stopping for donuts on the way home.

Do take your role as "family dietician" seriously.

Even if your kids don't *eat* all their meals at home, they do learn *how* to eat at home. Kids who hate a lot of healthy foods simply were not raised eating them, rather got accustomed to foods which appeal to our taste buds but are not healthy, such as those with sugar or deep fried.

Soft drinks, for example, are common in most family refrigerators. Completely eliminating them will be one huge step to changing how your kids eat. Point out how a soft drink is nothing but chemicals, or chemicals plus sugar. There is no health benefit, only damage to our bodies. Teach the benefits of proper hydration and accomplishing it with water.

Be familiar with and explain the revised "food pyramid" (heavy in vegetable and fruits), which is completely different from the same chart most parents were rasied with when they were children.

The simplest way to alter your child's eating behavior is to just stop buying certain products. If there are no soft drinks (or "sports" drinks which are often really just soft drinks—check their label) in the fridge, your kids will need to choose something else. You might want to even consider buying a good quality blender to make fruit and veggie smoothies. That is not only healthy, but lets kids be creative in coming up with the best smoothie recipes.

An important thing to remember, however, is to try to avoid conflicts about food if possible. For example, let's say you want your child to eat some fresh green vegetables. We all have taste preferences, so do you really care if your child will eat a cold spinach salad, but not eat lima beans? Or he or she will eat broccoli, but balks at Brussels sprouts? If fresh green vegetables are not part of your daily routine, have a few "taste nights," and see which "good foods" are going to be welcomed on a dinner plate and which are not, and simply make those vegetables instead.

How you prepare vegetables makes a big difference too. Many vegetables, when boiled, are soggy and mushy, and frozen and canned are never close to fresh in taste or nutrition. So experiment with how your family likes vegetables cooked. For most people, asparagus is best when grilled; broccoli or cauliflower lightly steamed for only 10-12 minutes. Other foods, like spinach, is usually best cold and raw with tasty toppings. (Kids see salads as "boring," but adding toppings can make a huge difference, including something crunchy like tortilla strips.)

If you are intent on your child eating a particular food, let's say the super-healthy choice of spinach, let your child know it's *going* to be on the dinner table tonight, but *they* get to choose how it is prepared. So at one sitting, give several tasting options. In front of them you have boiled frozen spinach (a big yuck for most of us, but intentionally there to make the other options look good by comparison, so don't exclude it—yes, you are not just a dietician but a psychologist too!), a cold spinach salad with a choice of toppings, and a smoothie option (perhaps equal parts raw fresh spinach and frozen mango chunks, ice and a wedge of lime to cut the strong spinach taste). Yes, it's green, but it tastes red!

Usually this will ensure that your child will not only accept one spinach option (just using spinach as an example), but actually embrace it. If your son or daughter is one of those kids who absolutely won't put anything green in their mouths, you might want to go with a playful "eyes closed smoothie taste test." Don't let them have anything sweet beforehand, like a soft drink, as that will make the smoothie taste less sweet. And if you make sure they are both hungry and thirsty for their taste test, all the better. Once they admit they like it, or at least don't hate it, the "green factor" usually goes away. Luckily, kids today, more so than past generations, are more conscious of the importance of healthy eating. Still, they want enjoy what they eat!

Don't feel you need to solve every problem.

Whether you hear it from your spouse, or directly from your child, you will be told of problems that your child is going through in that long and difficult voyage through childhood. It's a sad fact that kids can be particularly cruel toward each other, especially "girl on girl." The natural reaction for well-meaning parents is to provide a solution to the problem. And if it is the kind of a problem a parent can solve, great.

But usually it's the kind of upsetting situation that can't be avoided in a child's world, such as another child's hurtful comments, or being left out of some activities or friendships. This makes your heart ache for your child, but you know to insert yourself in every such situation will likely only be detrimental to your child down the road, particularly in their relationships with those other children they will have to interact with at school or in the neighborhood in the future.

Kids intuitively know this, and don't necessarily want you to try to make every problem go away. But you can absolutely help in several ways: 1) You can be the sympathetic listener; 2) You can teach empowerment; and 3) You can teach a healthy philosophy of life. These can all help not just now, but in the years ahead. Let's look at these three specific options:

A sympathetic and patient ear, listening without interruption, or a caring hug, is sometimes all a child really needs and wants. And you can show empathy by sharing a story about yourself at their age, when you went through the same thing. The unspoken words being, "I'm here and happy, so I survived it. So will you."

You also want to empower your child. A helpful lifelong philosophy to teach is "Don't let other people take your happiness away." The reality is that most "mean" people are secretly unhappy themselves, and this seems to motivate them to take happiness away from others.

Here is a way to show that just because someone says something does not make it true—and that in fact, those people are actually just plain wrong. As an example, use your child's favorite singers, let's say Taylor Swift and Katy Perry, and point out how great they are, but then go online together (YouTube comments, Twitter, et cetera) and see all the terribly cruel things some people say about them. Clearly those people are wrong and just because they said something does not make it true. And if Taylor Swift and Katy Perry listened to those comments, they would never be where they are.

Also, share the importance of your child's own inner strength and personal choices in how to react when things don't go as we want. Everyone in the world has asked "Why do bad things happen to good people?" Your child needs to know that he or she is not exempt from the "sometimes bad things happen in life" reality.

Every person, child or adult, wakes up with the option to be happy or sad. As Abraham Lincoln is credited with saying: *"You are as happy as you want to be."* This sounds like an overly simple "fortune cookie" philosophy, but it's actually brilliant.

We each have personal control whether we are happy or sad, despite what others may do or say to us. It's common for a child to think, "I'd be happy if only . . ." The "if only" might be having a certain friend, a new cell phone, the most popular jeans or tennis shoes, a car, less acne, et cetera. But we can demonstrate to our children how true happiness has nothing to do with popularity, beauty, having lots of possessions, or all the things we think dictate our happiness.

For example, you only need to look in the news to see how some of the youngest and most beautiful celebrities, who have everything a person could hope for in life, are clearly sad by their self-destructive behavior (drugs, suicide, arrests, repeated failed relationships). And to the contrary, there are people all over the world with barely enough to live on, and living a hard life, who start each day with a smile. Happiness and self-respect comes from inside ourselves and is a conscious decision.

Do we want to start our day with a smile or a frown? Do we want to be in control of our own emotional destiny, or let others control it for us? Helping your child embrace this philosophy, and see you living it as well, will go a long way toward them finding contentment not only as a child, but later as an adult as well.

Do consider lowering your standards for how clean your house must be.

It is one of the biggest and longest running conflicts in parent-child history: *"Clean your room! Pick up that mess! Who left the kitchen like this?"* It is exhausting for everyone and creates many negative emotions among family members.

The reality is that kids just don't see a "mess" the way you do. What is truly invisible to them is like a stick in the eye to most parents. This is not to say that teaching children the importance of some degree of cleanliness and order isn't expected, but as parents we sometimes go too far.

Remember, your house or apartment is your home, not a model house. Some kids feel that the appearance of the "model house" is more important to the parent than the child himself/herself. And when relatives or guests come to visit, there isn't excitement over their visit, it is the pressure of cleaning up the house before they arrive, so the visit almost has a negative undercurrent.

Here is a tale of two grown-up sisters: One was constantly telling her kids to "stay clean" and not get their clothes dirty while playing, and keeping a spotless house. She could rarely relax and really enjoy her home or family as she was so busy keeping everything perfect. Her sister had fun with her family and didn't stress about some degree of disorder in her home, that her kids played outside and got dirty doing so, or the fact someone left crumbs on the kitchen counter. When company came to visit she focused on them and her family, not the degree of cleanliness and order of the house. Who do you think was happier? Whose kids and spouse do you think was happier?

Many parents could learn to accept a degree of disorder and less than perfect cleanliness in their home. And when people come for a visit, resist the automatic, "Sorry, the place is such a mess," comment, when in fact it is a normal house, lived in by a normal family. Don't hold the standard of a model home, or those pictured in magazines, to your life. No one lives in those homes. You want your house to be a true home, which means it is lived in and enjoyed and used.

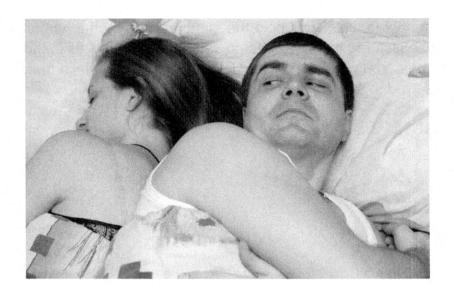

Do be prepared for the sex with your spouse to change.

When your sexual intimacy started with your spouse, it was pre-children, and you could focus solely on each other. But when you start your family, the realities of daily life come into play: jobs, meeting the needs of the kids, yard/house work, et cetera. Suddenly the sex diminishes and "family life" takes over.

Jealousy is not unknown when one parent might see the single-minded dedication that once went toward the spouse is now going to the child. If this occurs it is a wake-up call for both the parent feeling neglected (who might need to examine their self-esteem and maturity issues if they are jealous of affection going toward a child), and the parent who may be focusing too much on their child to the degree that their spouse feels neglected.

It is understandable that usually a couple's sex life will not match the key and vigorous role it played in the very beginning of the relationship. But still, as a relationship matures and adjusts, a happy marriage usually requires a happy bedroom. Early communication with each other about feeling neglected in the bedroom is key, whether this feeling comes from the husband or the wife. And talking specifically about bedroom desires should not be taboo.

Don't helicopter.

Helicopter parents are always hovering, watching out for any sign of a potential negative moment for their child. Making sure your child is safe is understandable, but being present at all times and desiring to protect them from every possible "bad" thing in their lives, is not.

Kids will have their challenging moments, some of them downright painful, but having a mom or dad there to keep them at bay, or instantly assuage the moment, is not serving the child's best interests in the long term. Remember, you will be there at home to hear about things your child needs to share, and to get involved in if that really proves to be necessary. But give your child the chance to experience and solve things first.

Don't worry about "spoiling" a child with love.

There is no such thing as giving a child too much love. When referring to "spoiling" a child, the problem is not too much love, rather it is giving *things* in place of love, usually because we are too busy to be the parent we want to be.

It *is* possible to smother a child with too much love and not give them the space they need to learn to grow and function as independent problem-solving people, but that is usually not a product of loving a child too much. This is more indicative of a parent's codependency with their child as a significant other (such as where the parent has few friends so their own child fills that void), or the parent has difficulties dealing with anxiety over a potential risks to which they imagine their child is vulnerable.

But simply giving your child "too much" love and affection is not going to "spoil" a child. In fact, the dedicated parent is more likely to be firm about behavior that is inappropriate, knowing that teaching good judgment and manners is an important part of their child's future success in life.

Don't defend yourself against every negative comment about you.

Children can say some incredibly cruel things, especially to the people they love the most, like their parents. If you want to find a good reason for this bad behavior, it's that your child feels secure enough in your love for him or her that they know they can safely say something terrible, as opposed to acting that way with a friend, who they know may reject them for such behavior.

The instinctive reaction is to defend yourself, and there might be times were that is appropriate. However, in many situations, the statement isn't even said with the true belief in the cruel words directed at you, rather frustration over a related situation, and you are the safe outlet. So again, there is a good side to their cruelty, that they trusted you enough to be their temporary whipping stone.

So rather than start your defense of yourself, consider saying, "I'm sorry you feel that way," then try to find out what is behind the anger.

Do teach good citizenship.

We've talked about the importance of being kind, and showing respect to others. But being nice and respectful isn't enough. You want your children to be part of the solution in making your city, your country and your planet a better place, and understanding that each of us has that responsibility?

A good thing to teach is, "One person can't change the world, but one person *can* make a difference in their own little part of the world, and if we all do that, we *can* change the world."

Your example is critical, in not just talking the talk, but walking the walk. There are many opportunities to help others and make the world a better place. If you are in a club or organization, there are usually events to benefit people in need. Your church might have dedicated days to clean the church grounds, or do a food drive. On holidays like Thanksgiving you can volunteer at a community organization to serve or prepare food for those less fortunate. You can do your own food drive by having your child collect unwanted cans and unopened boxes of food to donate to a local shelter.

If you can't find a group activity, you can still do something on your own. There are many organizations, like World Vision, where you can sponsor a child for a small monthly fee (and get their picture and written updates about their life). Maybe you have a neighbor who is a senior citizen or has a physical challenge, and offer to take their trash cans to the street that are too heavy for them. Or you and your child can be the ones who pick up the trash everyone stares at in the park or on your street but no one does anything about. And by the way, kids will always enjoy a charitable activity more if they are sharing it with other kids, so try to get other parents and kids involved.

An added benefit of encouraging your child to do these activities will enhance their feeling of self-worth. Strive to find a special activity at least once a year where you and your child are finding a cause to contribute your time and efforts.

Do keep a TV only in the living room, and try to avoid "screens" in everyone's bedrooms.

Watching movies or TV shows on television may not be as great as some other activities, but the reality is everyone wants to crash out and veg in front of the TV from time to time. What can make it a nice activity, however, is if you are doing it together, rather than everyone in their own room, staring at their own computer screens or TVs.

Especially as kids grow, their interests in entertainment will change, but there will always be some shows, movies or events that the whole family can enjoy together.

Be aware also that married couples that have a TV in their bedroom have intimacy less often that couples without one. And kids with TVs in their room, or who watch excessive shows on their computer, sleep less and are more likely to have an excessive unhealthy weight.

Don't "pass the buck" to the other parent.

There is a natural inclination to want to avoid making tough decisions, or where you know your answer will make your child mad at you. For example, your daughter wants to go out on her first date and you think she's not ready, or you have conditions. Or your son wants to spend the night at a friend's home where you don't feel good about the parental supervision, or the character of the other kids in attendance.

Particularly when you want to say "no," don't automatically answer your child's request with "Let me ask your mom/dad." This puts the burden on the other parent. And admit it, you are really stalling for time to deliver the "no," or you don't want to be the one to face your child's disappointment. Changing that just slightly to "Your mom/dad and I will talk about it," paints it as a shared decision, which is preferable.

Or you can say, "Let me think about it and we'll talk about it tomorrow." In this way you are taking primary responsibility. This is not to say your child can't know you will later be discussing the issue with the other parent, as that should be the case in all major parenting decisions, but you don't need to make the decision be seen as primarily that of the other parent. And if the answer to your child's request is "no," you can't be afraid to be the parent who delivers it.

Don't control your kids. Guide them.

Kids resent being told what to do, particularly when it feels to them it happens all day long: first at home, then at school, then later by a coach or after-school activities leader. Your goal as a parent is not simply to get your children to do what you want, rather to guide them to become self-motivated, high-functioning adults, respecting themselves and others, and eventually becoming a positive force in the world.

It is true that you may make your personal day easier by simply ordering your child to do certain tasks, at certain times, and in certain ways. ("You *will* do your homework the minute you get home from school and you will *not* get up from the dining room table until it's done. No friends, no TV.") But issuing such orders does not empower your child in any way, or truly teach responsibility, just how to follow orders.

Here's an example of how to encourage independent thinking rather than giving an order. Rather than say " Bring a jacket, it will get cold later," try a question: "Do you think it's going to get cold later?" And if that didn't work, then "Do you think you need a jacket?"

And if they make the wrong decision, let them bear the consequences. (They declined a jacket, so they will have to deal with being cold. They forgot their lunch yet again, so they will be hungry during lunchtime at school). And you will be extra wise to not bring up the bad decision later with an "I told you so." Instead say nothing and let the natural consequence from their decision be their lesson. Hopefully they will be more likely to listen the next time you ask a question intended to make them think for themselves, such as "Do you think you need a jacket?" or "If you do that activity will you be able to finish your homework by eight o'clock?"

Do recognize your child may show love in different ways at different times.

Some kids are more affectionate than others. Some say "I love you," as much to you as you do to them. You may be sad your child rarely says "I love you," especially in their self-conscious pre-teen and teen years. But everyone, and particularly children, shows their love and affection differently.

For example, you might be very verbal, and be used to a lot of giving and receiving of "I love you." But maybe your child is not so verbally oriented. Perhaps he or she feels more comfortable sitting on your lap and snuggling while reading a book. Or maybe it's not even physical. Perhaps it's dedicating time and making craft projects for you, or asking to share time with you in activities like doing homework together, or baking cookies.

Be grateful for any such signs of affection and don't demand that the child's method of showing affection matches yours.

Do use the fewest words possible.

As adults, we love to talk, and talk. And talk. So when we feel a child needs advice or information, we can't wait to share our wisdom. But kids, even older ones in their teens, need it short. Their interest tends to wane the more words are spoken. Worse of all, the intended message is diluted by all the excess words.

A good plan is to strive for a short answer, as in under one minute. And if they have questions about it, they'll ask, and you start the one-minute clock again. If they don't ask questions, you likely gave them what they needed to know.

Don't criticize a child for bad behavior, criticize the behavior itself.

When we criticize someone, especially kids, our message is often unfortunately interpreted as "You are bad," "You are a failure," or "You are a disappointment." So rather than words that say, "*You* were bad," try words that instead say, "Your *behavior* was bad."

Perhaps a bad report card is being discussed and you know the poor grades are from lack of effort, not a genuine inability to do better. So instead of "You are such a disappointment to get three Ds on your report card," consider, "These grades are disappointing. I don't think your effort and study habits were very good. Let's discuss how we can change that." The first statement is saying "You are a bad student," but the second is saying "Your study habits are bad." One is commenting on the person and one is addressing the behavior.

More examples: "Your room is too messy," rather than "You are messy." "You need to get your chores done today," rather than "You are so lazy."

Do respect a child's need for privacy and decorum.

You are a dad and your daughter is a rapidly developing teenager. When she was four she'd run naked in the backyard through the sprinklers. Now she's conscious of her body and wants privacy. Even though to you she's still your little girl, you need to understand and respect these desires for private bathroom time, and knocking and waiting for a "come in" before entering the child's bedroom.

And this also applies to the parents' bodies and manner of dress. Dad likes to wake up Saturday morning and make breakfast for the family in his tighty-whitey underwear. Or maybe mom likes to wear a little nightie around the house at night that leaves little to the imagination. Maybe that was fine when the kids were little, but as children get more attuned to sexuality, they may become uncomfortable with you being too casual with your dress. Respect the kids' feelings, even if you feel they are overly sensitive.

Don't feel every holiday must be spent together.

Almost every family has had battles over where to spend holidays. Different sets of relatives live far apart—mom's parents live in one state and dad's parents in another, so maybe that means having to choose only one to visit, or you manage to visit both, but it requires spending most of your holiday in your car or on airplanes. It'd be nice if everyone could come to your house to host major holidays so the issue is solved, but that's not always possible.

And what about vacations? Maybe part of your family, let's say Dad and son, want to go skiing, but Mom and daughter want a week of tennis, swimming and a day spa? Although it is certainly ideal for families to spend their vacations together, it doesn't make sense if part of your family is going to not enjoy their vacation focused on an activity they don't like, just to be close to the people they spend every day with normally. Plus, dragging along unwilling participants means not only will they not have fun, but they will likely take away everyone else's enjoyment as well.

It's perfectly fine to sometimes go your separate ways for holidays or vacations. With families often extended over great distances for holidays (especially if there are second marriages involved), and different interests to explore on vacations, it's just a reality. So wish each other well and enjoy your time each doing exactly what you want. When you are all back together at home again you all have a lot of stories and adventures to share. And think about it, if you are following the suggestions in this book, you are already spending a lot of quality time together, so there is no pressure to spend all of every vacation together as well.

From the Author

Thanks so much for reading *PARENTING: 50 One-Minute DOs & DON'Ts for Moms and Dads.* Taking the time to learn more about effective parenting shows how much you care about being the best possible parent. As the saying goes, "It takes a village to raise a child," but as parents we are the chiefs of that village.

If you have a comment or question, I'd enjoy hearing from you at Randy@RandallHicks.com. I respond to all emails. Perhaps you will even have a suggestion to improve a future edition of this book. (However, you don't need to write to me just to point out there are actually fifty-*one* DOs and DON'Ts. I just decided to sneak in one extra.☺)

Again, thanks for reading. I hope you will take a moment to review this book online on Amazon or other online retailer so others looking for help in parenting can hear from real people in finding helpful resources. One comment I've heard from many readers is that by the time they'd finished other parenting books, they had to struggle to remember more than one or two take-aways from it, but with this book they remembered several and had already "tested them" and found them effective. I sincerely hope that is the case for you, as my goal was to made this book fun, easily readable, with tips ready to instantly put into action.

Best wishes,

About the Author

Randall Hicks has written informational books regarding both parenting and family-formation, as well as several novels. He is the father of two children, now young adults. He is proud they are brave and self-confident people, living and working in foreign countries, one as an aspiring filmmaker in South America and one as an English teacher in Southeast Asia.

Randy's books have been featured on many national TV shows (*The Today Show, CBS This Morning, The Home Show, Sally Jesse Raphael, Mike & Maty, John and Leeza from Hollywood*, and more) as well as in the print media (*The New York Times, Chicago Sun Times, Los Angeles Times*, and more).

Randy's first education was at The University of Mom and Dad, and he will tell you he attended the world's best such university. Although he included psychology in his studies for his bachelor's, masters and doctorate degrees, he became an attorney, limiting his practice to adoption. Most of his life and career has been focused on children. He has served on the Board of Directors of a national charity focusing on the prevention of child abuse, pioneered a program distributing educational parenting materials in third-world countries, mentored youth offenders paroled from the California Youth Authority, taught Sunday School, been a 4-H group leader, coached high school sports, is the founder of JuniorTennisUSA (a YouTube channel where kids give all on-air instruction), and he was the host of *Adoption Forum*, a PBS mini-series that focused on parenting in adoption.

CPSIA information can be obtained
at www.ICGtesting.com
Printed in the USA
LVOW13s0327140717

541330LV00008B/158/P

9 780979 443053